	DATE DUE		
AP 12 '02			
AP 22 '02	JA 04 '06		
OC 08 '02	MAR 25 '08		
JA 08 '03	MAY 14 '08		
FE 20 '03	NOV 24 '08		
OC 30 '03	MAR 24 '09		
NO 18 '03	MAY 13 '09		
OC 06 '04	NOV 20 '09		
AP 21 '05	FEB 02 '10		
MY 12 '05	MAR 16 '10		
NO 09 '05			
DE 13 '06			

UNSOLVED MYSTERIES

the secret files

Ghosts and Poltergeists

Graham Watkins

the rosen publishing group's
rosen central

For the researchers in parapsychology

Published in 2002 by The Rosen Publishing Group, Inc.
29 East 21st Street, New York, NY 10010

First Edition

Library of Congress Cataloging-in-Publication Data

Watkins, Graham.
Ghosts and poltergeists / by Graham Watkins.
p. cm. — (Unsolved mysteries)
Includes bibliographical references and index.
Summary: Discusses some real-life cases of ghosts and hauntings, as well as some of the theories about them.
ISBN 0-8239-3563-9
1. Ghosts—Juvenile literature. 2. Haunted houses—Juvenile literature. [1. Ghosts. 2. Haunted houses.] I. Title. II. Unsolved mysteries (Rosen Publishing Group)
BF1461 .W35 2002
133.1—dc21

2001003787

Manufactured in the United States of America

Contents

Introduction

Ghosts, hauntings, and poltergeists have been a part of the beliefs of people all over the world since the beginning of recorded history. Movies about ghosts and haunted houses, such as *The Haunting* and *Poltergeist,* continue to draw large audiences even in our age of computers and high-tech marvels. But do people still actually believe in such things as hauntings? Maybe not, because you often hear people say, "There's no such thing as a ghost."

In fact, though, there exist places in even the most modern cities where, at times, things happen that defy ordinary scientific explanation. Are ghosts really responsible for mysterious knockings? Do mysterious cold spots mark the sites of murders? Are there truly such things as haunted houses?

There is now a branch of science that studies exactly those phenomena. It is called parapsychology. Scientific parapsychology began in Cambridge, England, in 1882, when the Society for Psychical

The study of ghosts and hauntings centers on strange occurrences in old houses.

Research was established. Experimental parapsychology began in the 1930s when J. B. Rhine established the Department of Parapsychology at Duke University in Durham, North Carolina. This department later became the Institute for Parapsychology. Research subjects for parapsychologists include ghosts, hauntings, and poltergeists.

None of these scientists would say, "There's no such thing as a ghost." For them a ghost might not be exactly what it has always been thought to be, but sometimes they come upon some truly strange occurrences in old houses and castles thought to be haunted.

Ghosts and spirits are described by people who claim to have seen them as having an unclear, out-of-focus appearance.

1

What Is a Ghost?

Everyone knows what a ghost is. It's the spirit of a person who has died, a spirit that for some reason remains here on Earth instead of "going on" to wherever the dead go.

That's perhaps the most common belief concerning ghosts—not just in our modern society, but among different peoples around the world and throughout history. For example, some Native American tribes believed that the spirit of a person who had been scalped could not rest unless certain rituals took place. If these rituals weren't performed, or weren't done correctly, the ghost would linger and be very troublesome to the tribe. In Christian belief, the souls of people who have died are not expected to remain among the living—and if they do, people question why they have not "gone on" as they were supposed to.

The reasons, as anyone who has ever read a ghost story or seen a movie about ghosts can tell you, usually have to do with either the way people died or with events that took place in their lives or the lives of their loved ones. Ghosts are often portrayed as seeking revenge against their murderers. Sometimes ghosts are said to linger on Earth because of "unfinished business," like paying for some crime they committed or protecting loved ones. Finally, it sometimes seems that the ghosts have simply claimed a house for their own purposes and are trying to drive intruders away.

In many tales, ghosts are associated with specific places we describe as "haunted." Although almost any place, from a building to a car, can be considered haunted, we tend to think first of a house when we hear the

Ghosts can live in many different places, as suggested in the movie *Ghost*.

word "haunted." The traditional image of a haunted house is usually an old and run-down home in which no one lives.

A haunted house—or any other haunted place—is actually a place where things happen that do not seem to have any natural or scientific explanation, at least as far as the people observing those happenings are concerned. Often enough, these strange occurrences are not associated with any known story about a ghost. At the moment, no one knows whether a ghost is necessary to cause a haunting, since we do not know with any certainty what ghosts or hauntings are.

One special type of ghost, which produces a special type of haunting, is known as a poltergeist. The word itself is German, meaning "mischievous ghost"—although, as we shall see, poltergeists are probably something very different from ghosts. The most common cases of poltergeist activities involve objects moving about for no apparent reason. Sometimes the objects actually fly around, at times with dangerous force. For example, a glass may suddenly zoom off a table and shatter against a nearby wall.

One type of poltergeist causes spontaneous fires.

Parapsychologists have also named special kinds of poltergeists. One that has been reasonably well identified is known as the firestarter. In these cases, objects seem to catch fire for no obvious reason. Another type of poltergeist is called the water poltergeist. In these cases, pools of water may appear in odd places—again, without any apparent reason.

2

Ghosts and Haunted Houses

Haunted houses—or, more properly, haunted places—exist all over the world. In almost every town there is a place that local residents consider haunted. Some of these haunted houses aren't haunted at all. They are merely old places that have a spooky look about them, or have had some local legend attached to them.

In many other cases—and these cases account for a large number of so-called hauntings—odd things do happen. However, after careful investigation of each case, many, and sometimes all, of these events blamed on ghosts are found not to be odd at all.

Case One: The Tennessee House

The people who were renting an old house in eastern Tennessee were convinced that it was haunted. Practically everyone who entered said that it "looked strange" or that they "felt strange," although no one could say why. The renters complained of doors opening when they had been closed tightly and of objects such as chairs moving on their own. In one case, as reported by the renters, this resulted in a wooden chair dramatically falling down a flight of stairs when no one was upstairs—an event taken by them as proof that the house was indeed haunted. One man swore he had been "attacked" by the furnace, an old-style coal-burning heater. He said he had gone to put fresh coal in it after the fire had gone out, only to have flames roar out at him as soon he opened the door.

The mystery of this aggressive furnace was the easiest one to solve—the air ducts had not been cleaned and were blocked with cinders. Although the fire had gone out and the outside of the furnace was cold to the touch, heat remained down in the bed of coals. The fire had stopped burning because the coals were

The case of the "attacking furnace" was solved by the logical explanation of clogged ventilation ducts.

no longer exposed to oxygen—fires can't burn without oxygen. When the man opened the door, fresh air rushed in. Naturally, the fire roared back to life.

The other mysteries concerning this house were a little more difficult to solve, but some measurements with a protractor gave the answer. The walls were not quite at right angles—90 degrees—to the floors and ceilings. They were, however, very close to 90 degrees. The one farthest off was at 92 degrees. These small differences are very difficult for the human eye to catch. They just look somehow wrong. It is well known that a building with angles just off from 90 degrees makes a person feel odd. A number of "mystery houses" promoted as tourist attractions take advantage of this effect.

This slight "wrongness" was also what caused the doors to open. The door frames were not truly squared, and as a result, the doors, when closed, were under stress, causing them to pop open without warning. The moving objects the renters had mentioned were probably caused by the fact that none of the floors were level, and items, including that dramatically falling chair, were simply sliding downhill.

Case Two: Seashells from the Sky

If a certain house in eastern North Carolina was actually haunted, it was a very unusual type of haunting. According to both the woman who lived there and her neighbors who witnessed the strange happenings, the house was haunted not by a ghost—but by seashells.

The woman said that, at times, seashells fell from the sky like rain. Sometimes they even fell inside the house. Investigators found that her yard and her roof were literally covered with seashells; the rain gutters were filled with them. Even stranger, the seashells apparently fell only on her property. Neighboring yards showed only a few, which might have been kicked there or moved by water from ordinary rainstorms. The shells themselves were quite ordinary as well. They were sun-bleached clam and cockle shells, which can be collected by the truckload along the North Carolina shore, which is some eighty miles away.

Since the investigators never saw any shells fall on or around the house, this case rests only on the testimony of the woman and her neighbors. Of course it could have been faked—though why anyone would go to the trouble to truck in tons of

The case in which tons of seashells fell on a single property was never explained.

seashells and dump them on and around the woman's house remains a mystery.

"Rains" of various sorts of things—fish and frogs are the most common—are called Fortean phenomena after researcher Charles Fort, who recorded and cataloged thousands of such occurrences. We know today that rains of fish, frogs, and similar items are sometimes caused by tornadoes, which occasionally suck up whole ponds along with their contents and drop them in some other place when the tornadoes disappear.

Why tornadoes would drop seashells on this woman's property and on her property alone, not in the neighbors' yards, would be very difficult to explain.

And then there are some houses—not very many, but a few—that are almost impossible to explain.

Case Three: The Kentucky House

It is called simply the Kentucky House in the records, because the owners of the property were very reluctant to have the house publicly known as "haunted."

An investigation of the Kentucky House took place in January, 1970. The house had not been occupied for approximately eighty years. It was a large house, of a style associated with the plantation homes of the pre–Civil War South. When it was abandoned, practically all of the furnishings and other household items were left in it. When the house was investigated, the rooms were all still furnished, down to the dishes in the kitchen and the books on the shelves in the library. In eighty years, these things had only occasionally been disturbed, so they all remained as they were—except for being covered with a truly amazing amount of dust.

Almost every old house has the look of being haunted.

In legend and tradition, the haunting of the Kentucky House began when the young couple for whom it was built spent their wedding night there. They had, so it is said, a terrible fight. What the fight was about no one knows, since neither of them survived that night. According to tradition and to some reports in old newspapers, the argument ended in tragedy—the young man murdered his bride for an unknown reason, and then, overcome with remorse, committed suicide. Tradition holds that the young woman was murdered in an upstairs bedroom and that her husband killed himself in the kitchen. There has not been independent verification of this, however.

There were also stories about how people had tried to spend nights in this house over the decades, and how some of them had died there. Few of these tales were verifiable, but it was said that there were only two causes of death—heart attacks and injuries caused by falling down the curving staircases that led up from each side of the front room on the first floor to the second floor.

One of the best-known oddities associated with the house was a "cold spot" located in one of the upstairs bedrooms. This reportedly was the scene of the murder. The cold spot, an area about three feet in diameter located near the center of the room, actually did feel much cooler than the rest of the room, but measurements with thermometers showed no difference in temperature between this area and the warm areas around it. Measurements of relative humidity showed no differences either, and there were no drafts to account for the feeling of cold in this spot.

In science, subjective feelings, or the "gut reactions" of an investigator, are not good enough. Instead, some sort of objective outside measure is needed. It was decided in this case to bring animals into the cold spot to see if they would react. But the tests were not conclusive. Lab rats showed no reaction. But lab rats have lost much of their natural instincts, and do not even recognize predators like snakes as dangerous. However, when a cat was brought into the house, she went into a panic from the moment she entered until she was removed.

The next animal brought into the house was a rattlesnake. It was hoped that the snake, being cold-blooded, might become lethargic when exposed to the spot, which would demonstrate that it too felt the "cold," and try to move toward the warmer area outside the cold spot.

Instead, the snake immediately drew itself into a defensive coil and began to rattle. This in itself was very unusual, since this snake had been in captivity for many years and did not rattle at people outside its cage. Even more surprising was that it moved its head from side to side as if following something unseen outside the cage. At least twice it drew its head back sharply, as a frightened snake does when an enemy approaches it closely. Since this was objective evidence of something unusual taking place in the house, the investigation continued.

By day, there was nothing unusual (other than the cold spot) to be seen, heard, or felt in this house. After dark, though, the house became very noisy. Most of the noises sounded like footsteps or someone banging a fist against walls or, more

An investigator stayed two nights inside the Kentucky House library, much like the one seen here.

commonly and more dramatically, against doors. These sounds seemed to come from all over the house.

On the first evening of the investigation, there was no sense that whatever was producing the noises was interested in or even aware of the investigator, who stayed in the library most of the night. A book pushed out from the shelf, stopping just short of dropping onto the floor. The investigator, after making some notes, pushed it back into place—and it promptly slid out again, almost as if there was a spring behind it. The book was removed, and there was nothing behind it, but when it was replaced it again slid out—though not quite as far. Over the next thirty to forty-five minutes the investigator pushed it back into place repeatedly, and although it kept sliding out again, it moved a shorter distance each time until the effect finally disappeared.

The investigator kept a tape recorder running continuously throughout the night, and as close to the hour as possible, spoke time markers into the microphone: "It is now eleven o'clock," "It is now 1:06 AM." At times, the noises in the house were so loud that the investigator wondered if his time markers would be audible.

But later, when the tape was reviewed, it was found that while the time markers were loud and clear, most of the noises from the house could not be heard at all. Only a few sounds were recorded, and these were usually scraping sounds like that of furniture being moved. In a few places tracks in the dust suggested that furniture had been moved, but none was ever actually seen in motion. In other words, whatever most of those sounds were, they did not affect the tape recorder's microphone—just as the coldness of the spot in the bedroom did not affect a thermometer.

What this suggests is that these noises were not sounds at all, not in terms of the definition of a sound as a vibration of the air. The investigator seemed to be hearing them—certainly he would have sworn in any courtroom that he had heard them—but the evidence of the tape recorder suggests that he did not.

Late in the evening of his second night in the house, the investigator, who was again in the library, was startled by one of the loud bangs that sounded like someone hitting a door with a fist—only this time, the blow was delivered against one of the library doors. At that point, just for an instant, the investigator lost his scientific objectivity as an observer and was at least a little frightened.

Then things changed dramatically. For a moment, the house went completely silent. Then suddenly all the sounds started again—the bangings, the footsteps, low moaning sounds, noises like distant voices saying words that could not be understood. But instead of being scattered at random around the house, they all seemed to be concentrated around the library. It was as if the house had become aware of the investigator's presence for the first time.

The investigator, feeling that he might now be in some real danger, decided to call off the observation and leave. As he made his way down the hallway toward the stairs, the sounds seemed to follow him, echoing out of the mostly closed rooms he was passing. At the top of the stairs, the investigator suddenly remembered all the stories about people who had died from falls here, and, despite being in a hurry, forced himself to hold the banister tightly as he began to descend.

This proved to be an excellent decision. Two or three steps from the top, the investigator's foot caught on something that felt like a wire or thin rope stretched across the stairs. If he had not been holding the banister, he would have been sent hurtling headfirst down the steps. There was nothing visible on the stair, however.

Now in more of a hurry than ever to get out of the house, the investigator went down the stairs as quickly as possible. He had just reached the front door and was opening it when he felt a hand grab at the back of his neck. The fingers slipped off, as if whatever had grabbed at him had almost gotten him but just missed.

The investigator didn't bother to look back to see what was there. He hurried outside and did not return for his equipment until noon of the following day. At that point he decided to wait for a few weeks or months before trying to stay in the house at night again.

Before any further experiments could be done, however, the owners of the property had the house demolished. There has never been any evidence that the site on which it stood is now in any sense haunted.

Miscellaneous Cases

It's not always possible to say whether something unusual has happened in a supposedly haunted house. The residents—and sometimes the local officials, such as police officers and priests—may tell spectacular stories about ghosts and strange happenings, but researchers, when they visit, see nothing. Many apparent hauntings fall into this category: houses or places where weird or supernatural things are said to have happened, but offer nothing that can be documented scientifically.

Some of these incidents occurred in places that might be expected to be haunted. For example, there have been dozens of reports of ghosts inhabiting the famous Tower of London, where hundreds of people were killed or executed over the centuries.

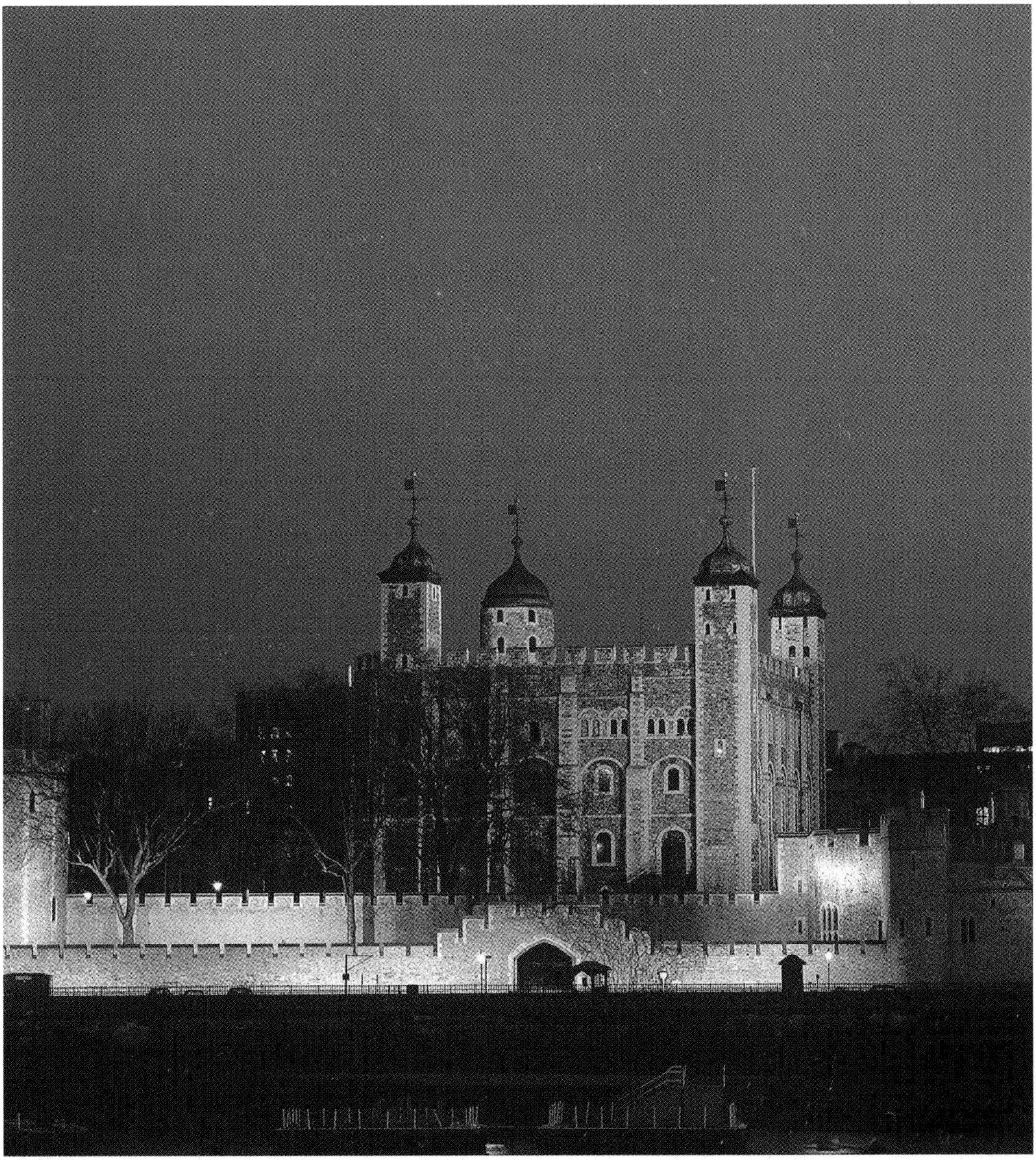

As the site of hundreds of executions, the Tower of London plays host to many ghost stories.

Some of these ghosts are said to be those of famous people. Many visitors to the Tower have reported sightings of the ghosts of Anne Boleyn, Lady Jane Grey, and Mary, Queen of Scots. Sometimes ghosts are not seen or imagined, but local people tell stories of odd noises or changes in temperature.

At other times the ghosts are apparitions of a very different sort. Abbey House in Cambridge, England, is said to be haunted by two ghosts. One appears to be a nun, but the other seems to be an animal, a strange creature described as looking like a large rabbit but with short ears, and which runs about on two legs like a person. At least two families who occupied this house at different times have reported seeing this odd animal running through the house. What is it? No one knows.

Some Tower of London visitors swear they have seen the ghost of Lady Jane Grey, beheaded for treason in 1554.

3

Poltergeists

Although the poltergeist (mischievous ghost) is sometimes considered to be a special kind of ghost, all the evidence we have now suggests that it is really something different. Unlike ghosts, poltergeists usually infest ordinary homes where ordinary families live. They most often appear in families with a child or children near the age of puberty, or children who are overly angry or anxious.

In several cases, investigators have actually observed poltergeist activity in such homes. Dr. William G. Roll, formerly of the Psychical Research Foundation in Durham, North Carolina, has done extensive studies on poltergeists, and two of his cases are noteworthy.

Case One: Olive Hill, Kentucky

The Callihan family was being troubled by objects flying about their home, glass breaking, furniture being overturned, and so on. They left their house for a time in an attempt to escape the poltergeist, but it seemed to follow them.

A researcher directly observed at least two strange incidents. Dr. Roll's associate, John Stump, saw glassware sliding across a counter on one occasion, and on another he saw a chair flip completely over. Later, while in the company of one of the family's five children—twelve-year-old Roger Callihan—Dr. Roll saw a kitchen table suddenly leap into the air, turn partially around, and land on the backs of the chairs that had been placed around it, ending up with all four of its legs off the floor.

Case Two: Bronx, New York

The poltergeist that disturbed the Robbins family in 1974 was very similar. Pictures would fall from the walls, lamps would fly off tables, and furniture would overturn. In one incident witnessed by researcher William Eisner, just after eight-year-old Ann Robbins went to bed, a loud crash was heard from her bedroom. When Eisner and the girl's parents went in, they found that Ann's desk and chair had overturned. She was on the far side of the bed undressing. The furniture was righted and the adults left. Three minutes later there was another crash—the desk had overturned again. Eisner noted that the girl's bedroom door was not closed and his line of sight was such that he would have seen her if she had attempted to dart around the bed and turn over the desk herself.

An interesting aspect of the Bronx case was the way in which objects that had moved once seemed likely to move again. Pictures fell from Mrs. Robbins's wall. She hung them back up, and they fell again. One night she observed a chair leaning against a wall and put it back on all four legs. The next day Mr. Robbins and a neighbor found the chair again balancing itself on two legs, the other two suspended in the air. He had to push it back down on the floor.

A number of people witnessed the poltergeist activity in the Robbins house, including several neighbors and a policeman who saw Ann's desk chair fall over when no one else was in the room.

In some cases, as in the Callihan case in Olive Hill, Kentucky, poltergeists seemed to follow a family if they tried to move away to escape the disturbances. This happened in a

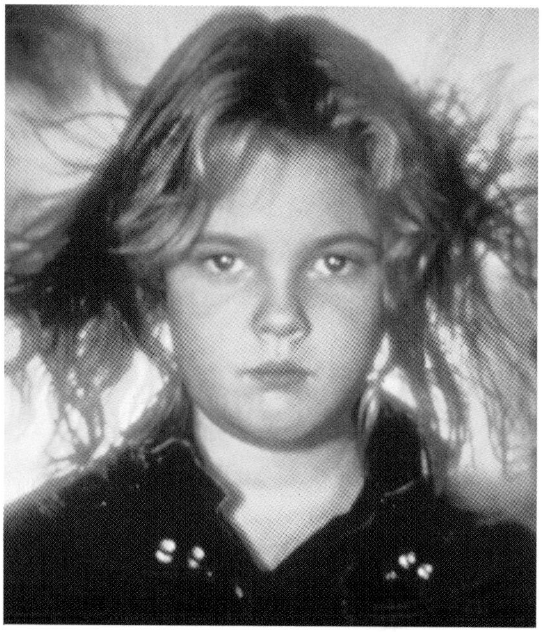

The power to start fires spontaneously is explored in the movie *Firestarter*, starring Drew Barrymore.

case in Bedford, Massachusetts, when the family being tormented by a poltergeist went to a motel only to have the activity start there, too.

The activity may linger in the house once the original family is gone, as if it were a haunting. The researcher Nandor Fodor has reported a case revolving around a fourteen-year-old girl in which the poltergeist activity continued in the house where the girl had lived, even after another family had moved in.

Special types of poltergeists, such as the firestarter and the water poltergeist, are more rare and have been observed much less frequently by investigators. There has never been a reliable case of anyone who was actually able to start fires at will, like the main character in the book and film *Firestarter*. This type of focused ability remains only in the realm of fiction.

4

Theories

So far, we have not yet considered what answers the investigators can give us for these phenomena. Unfortunately, there are not as many answers as we'd like, and even now all we can do is speculate.

In the discussion of the investigation of the Kentucky House in chapter 2, it was mentioned that instruments like thermometers could not be used to measure things like the cold spot in the bedroom, and that the noises the investigator heard could not be heard on the tape recording.

This type of phenomenon is not unusual. Studies show that people believe they can see strong magnetic fields, usually as a purple glow, and continue seeing it even if a solid wall is placed between the magnetic field and the viewer. But a camera does not record any glow. In fact, the person is not seeing the magnetic field at all. He or she feels the field—which is strong enough to move the iron in blood—but has no natural point of reference for the sensation since magnetic fields this powerful rarely occur outside a laboratory. So he or she interprets the unfamiliar sensation as "seeing" rather than "feeling."

It is possible that some of the sounds in so-called haunted houses are the same false sensation. The person "hearing" the sounds is feeling something for which his or her brain has no point of reference, and therefore he or she interprets those feelings as noises, or in other cases, as cold spots. The same sort of phenomenon may account for cases where ghosts are "seen" but cannot be photographed.

In the early 1970s, a series of experiments was performed at the Institute for Parapsychology in Durham to test for psychic healing ability in some people. The results were published in the *Journal of Parapsychology* and in *Research in Parapsychology*. In these studies, pairs of white lab mice were anesthetized with ether. The task of the human subject was to physically wake up one of the mice by using just his or her mind before its companion (called the control mouse), could awaken naturally. These studies were highly successful. The subjects were indeed able to awaken their mice much faster than the control mice awoke on their own.

To add to the fairness of the experiments, the experimenters who were handling the mice didn't know which of the two mice they were watching was being "worked on" by the human subject. The two mice were in small plastic pans on either side of a divider on a wooden table, and the human subject was on the other side of a one-way glass. Each experiment was divided into two parts, and at the break, the human subject would change sides, so that any outside effect—such as drafts—would be canceled out.

The experimenters noticed early on that the human subjects did not do very well with the trials that took place right after they had changed sides. A series of experiments was then done in which the subjects concentrated on one side and then left the laboratory after the break, while the experimenters continued to put etherized mice on the table as if the human subject was still there.

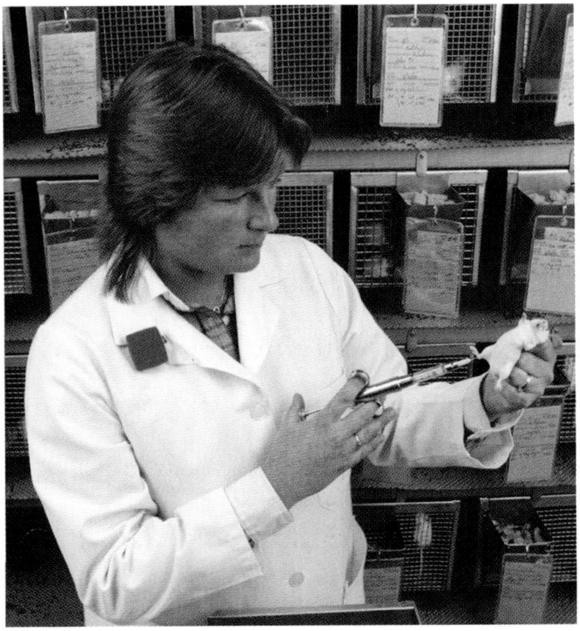

Lab mice are sometimes used in paranormal scientific experiments.

The results were most interesting. The mice on the side that had been "worked on" by the human subject continued to wake up faster than the control mice—as if whatever energy was being used to wake them up was lingering in some way. Even more interesting was that the patterns in the first half of the experiment persisted into the second half, when there was no subject. For example, if the subject had been waking up his or her mice very fast at first and then less dramatically toward the end of the half, the second half would follow the same pattern. A large number of these studies were performed, and the results were so dramatic that the odds of this linger effect happening by chance were one in billions.

This means that not only did some sort of energy linger, but in some way, information about what had happened in the first half of the trial persisted into the second half. During these studies, it was found that the effects lasted for about thirty minutes—just about the same length of time that the book in the Kentucky House kept pushing itself out from the shelf.

Two other findings from the mouse-ether series of experiments are important to our discussion. It was found that the human subjects showed elevated heart rates and lowered skin resistance, a response that scientists call the General Adaptation Syndrome, which is the state your body goes into when you are angry, frightened, or excited. Subjects who couldn't wake the mice were found not to be in this state. When they were trained to go into that state by using biofeedback, they were able to perform almost as well as the naturally successful subjects.

The other discovery was just as interesting. The wooden table being used had a metal supporting plate. Grounding this plate—simply attaching a wire from it to a nearby water pipe—completely stopped the human subjects, even those who had been successful before, from having any effect on the mice.

Wood does not conduct electricity. A metal plate like the one under the table does, and so does the body of an animal or a person. When you put two pieces of conducting material on either side of an insulator (a material which does not conduct electricity), you have made a capacitor, a device that can store electrical energy. However, if one of those conductors is grounded, the energy can drain away.

These studies seem to indicate that the force used to wake the mice behaves in the same way that electrical energy does. This force, however, is not simple electrical energy, since it cannot be detected by the use of an electroscope.

So how does this apply to hauntings and ghosts? If the stories about the wedding night murder in the Kentucky House are true, then the people involved were certainly feeling the effects of the General Adaptation Syndrome at the time of the tragedy—great anger for one, and great fear for the other. This could have led to a release of huge amounts of the same sort of energy used to wake up the mice.

That the house was old—more than 100 years old at the time it was demolished—means that it was built originally without plumbing or electrical service. In many old houses, plumbing and wiring were added later; pipes do not run under the houses much, and the wiring is ungrounded. A modern house by contrast has electrical grounds all through and under it—and this might well explain why haunted houses tend to be old structures. In newer houses the energy does not remain because there are electrical grounds to drain it away. The fact that this force seems to be "programmable" in some way—as we have seen in the mouse-ether experiments—means that these old structures could retain patterns related to whatever caused the haunting in the first place for a very long time.

Another possibility—and this is just as likely—is that the energy does not carry a "pattern" of this sort at all, but may be in some way directed by the living people in the house. This means that if they are frightened, the energy might show itself as threatening—in other words, giving them what they expect. The fact that the Kentucky House did not seem to "notice" the investigator until he was frightened makes this a real possibility.

Some current research makes this second theory of hauntings seem even more likely. Dr. Roll, mentioned earlier, discovered that a number of haunted houses seem to show electrical or magnetic disturbances. These may have been caused by the haunting or they may have come before it, making it possible for that particular structure to become haunted in the first place. As yet, we do not know enough to say much about it.

The electrical energy in a room can cause people to think they see an aura, which many people think is a ghost.

Poltergeists, based on research into them, do indeed seem to be very different. You may have noticed in the cases mentioned in chapter 3 that each one involved a family with children who were just reaching or had just passed puberty. In fact, this is the most common feature of poltergeist activities—they seem to always center on a child. In several of the cases the children involved have been examined by child psychologists and were found to have some psychological problems—they are usually overly angry or anxious.

The theory that scientists have put forward is that these troubled children, with all their pent-up emotions, are causing the poltergeist activity themselves with psychokinesis—the movement of objects by the force of the mind alone. That is why poltergeist activity is referred to in scientific literature as RSPK, or recurrent spontaneous psychokinesis.

These abilities are not under the child's control. In fact, the child in question normally does not even know that he or she is causing the activity. This, of course, is why the activity often follows a family when they move out of a house to escape the disturbances—since they take their children with them, they are taking the cause with them as well.

Of course, there are a few "poltergeist cases" where a child has been caught creating the disturbances by ordinary physical means, such as magnets or strings rigged to pull things over. These "cases" have a different name: fake!

Conclusions

What can we conclude from all these cases, and from all the research done on ghosts and poltergeists? Do we finally know all the secrets about ghosts and hauntings?

No, we most certainly do not. With all the scientific research that has been done, we still don't know exactly what those things we call ghosts and poltergeists are. The research into the causes of hauntings continues, but for now, the ghosts seem to be holding onto their secrets very well. And if you should happen to encounter a ghost and it seems to be threatening you, the best advice we can give you is to find a water pipe and stand over it! You may then "short out" any electrical phenomena.

If the ghost remains despite that . . . well, all we can recommend then is that you'll have your very own chance to investigate a secret file!

Glossary

anesthetize To render an animal or person unconscious with a drug, usually for the purpose of surgery.

capacitor An electrical device consisting of two conductive plates separated by an insulator; used to store electrical energy.

control The part of a scientific experiment to which nothing is done; used for comparison with the other part or parts.

electroscope A device consisting of two metal leaves that spread in the presence of an electrical field (because both get the same electrical charge and like charges repel each other).

firestarter Term for a type of poltergeist activity that involves unexplained fires.

Fortean phenomena Odd and unexplained occurrences that do not fit known categories. The term comes from the name of a documenter of such occurrences, Charles Fort.

General Adaptation Syndrome A series of biological events that occur in the body of an animal or person to ready it for strenuous activity.

ghost An unexplained apparition usually thought to be the spirit of a deceased person.

ground Electrical term for the charge of the earth itself, used as an electrical reference point.

haunting Unexplained sights, sounds, smells, or other sensations that occur regularly over a period of time in a specific location.

linger effect In parapsychology, a term that describes the persistence of a paranormal phenomenon in or on a certain place.

paranormal Phenomena that are inexplicable in terms of our ordinary understanding or current scientific knowledge.

parapsychology A term coined by Dr. J. B. Rhine to describe the scientific study of all paranormal processes, including psychokinesis, ghosts, and so on.

poltergeist A "mischevious ghost" responsible for unexplained noises, movements of objects, outbreaks of fires, or floods. Poltergeist activity usually centers on a person, rather than a place.

psychokinesis Influencing physical things (moving objects, for example) with the power of the mind alone.

RSPK Recurrent spontaneous psychokinesis; the technical term for the poltergeist.

For More Information

American Society for Psychical Research, Inc.
5 West 73rd Street
New York, NY 10023
(212) 799-5050
Web site: http://www.aspr.com

Parapsychology Foundation, Inc.
228 East 71st Street
New York, NY 10021
(212) 628-1550
Web site: http://www.parapsychology.org/dynamic/splash/index.cfm

The Rhine Research Center
Institute for Parapsychology
402 N. Buchanan Boulevard
Durham, NC 27701-1728

(919) 688-8241
Web site: http://www.rhine.org

Web Sites

Scientific Sites:

Are Phantasms Fact or Fantasy?
http://www.boundaryinstitute.org/articles/PhantasmJSPR.pdf

The Committee for the Scientific Investigation of Claims of the Paranormal
http://www.csicop.org/about/
A group devoted to "debunking" paranormal phenomena

The Koestler Parapsychology Unit at the University of Edinburgh
http://moebius.psy.ed.ac.uk/js_index.html

The Mystica: Poltergeist
http://www.themystica.com/mystica/articles/p/poltergeist.html

Parapsychology Resources on the Internet
http://www.roma1.infn.it/rog/group/frasca/b/parap.html

Psychic Science.com
http://www.mdani.demon.co.uk/para/parapsy.htm

Fun Sites

Evansville Courier & Press Ghost Cam
http://www.courierpress.com/ghost/

The Shadowlands
http://theshadowlands.net/

The X Chronicles
http://www.xzone-radio.com/xchronicles/v1n3.html

For Further Reading

Flammarion, Camille. *Haunted Houses.* New York: D. Appleton & Co., 1924.

Rogo, D. Scott. *An Experience of Phantoms.* New York: Taplinger, 1974.

Roll, William. G. *The Poltergeist.* New York: Doubleday, 1972.

The editors of Time-Life Books. *The Enchanted World: Ghosts.* Alexandria, VA: Time-Life Books, 1984.

The editors of Time-Life Books. *The Enchanted World: Tales of Terror.* Alexandria, VA: Time-Life Books, 1987.

Tyrrell, G. N. M. *Apparitions.* London: Duckworth & Co., 1953.

Index

About the Author

Graham Watkins is a former researcher at J. B. Rhine's parapsychology laboratory in Durham, North Carolina. Now a novelist and screenwriter, he has published five novels (*Dark Winds,* 1989; *The Fire Within,* 1991; *Kaleidoscope Eyes,* 1993; *Virus,* 1995; and *Interception,* 1997). He has also published more than fifteen pieces of short fiction. His works are available in six languages. He still lives in Durham with his wife and seventeen-year-old son, and is an editor for FireDance Literary Works of Atlanta.

Photo Credits

Cover © Bettman/Corbis; pp. 5, 6 © The Image Bank; pp. 8, 30 © The Everett Collection; p. 10 © EyeWire; pp. 12, 26, 29 © Bettman/Corbis; pp. 15, 17, 20, 25 © SuperStock; p. 33 © PhotoDisc; p. 37 © FPG International.

Series Design and Layout

Geri Giordano